one to one
BIBLE READING

a simple guide for every Christian
DAVID HELM

SYDNEY · YOUNGSTOWN

Matthias Media
(St Matthias Press Ltd ACN 067 558 365)
Email: info@matthiasmedia.com.au
Internet: www.matthiasmedia.com.au
Please visit our website for current postal and telephone contact information.

Matthias Media (USA)
Email: sales@matthiasmedia.com
Internet: www.matthiasmedia.com
Please visit our website for current postal and telephone contact information.

ISBN 978 1 921441 98 1

Cover design and typesetting by Lankshear Design.

What people are saying about
One-to-One Bible Reading

One-to-One Bible Reading is practical and clear. Our pastoral team is excited about how this resource will equip people to use Scripture to both evangelize and disciple. It's a tool we want every member of our church to have.

Joshua Harris
Senior Pastor of Covenant Life Church and author of *Dug Down Deep*

This is a fresh approach to one of the most practical and personal ways of sharing the gospel. This strategy for evangelistic ministry is very important for making disciples. Pastors, you'll want to get copies for your elders, deacons, staff, discipleship coordinators and congregations.

Justin Holcomb
Director of the Resurgence and Pastor at Mars Hill Church in Seattle

David Helm has written a guide to help Christians in one of the most basic methods of helping others: reading the Bible with them. In evangelism, in edification, nothing can beat opening the text of the Bible and reading what God himself has actually said. Christians need only have confidence in God's word and a basic skill in reading it with others. David has done us a great service in helping people gain that basic skill.

Phillip Jensen
Bible teacher and evangelist at Two Ways Ministries

One of my great joys in ministry among women is reading the Bible with just one other person. David's book explains in a clear and straightforward way how each one of us can get started in this simple yet life-changing ministry. If you have a heart for kingdom growth then read this book, pray and make a start!

Jenny Salt
Dean of Students at Sydney Missionary and Bible College

One-to-one Bible reading is vital for effective and vibrant gospel ministry. This simple guide to an essential ministry is a magnificent resource that will be useful for training all Christians in ministry. There is little else like it. We shall use it extensively at St Helen's.

William Taylor
Rector at St Helen's Bishopsgate in London

Helm's booklet encourages relational evangelism and discipleship based on the living and active word of God, offering practical tools for one-on-one Bible reading and envisioning a mobilization of God's people that would complement church programs. Helm calls us to invite people not only to an event, but into our lives and into the life of faith in Jesus Christ offered in his word.

Kathleen Nielson
Author and conference speaker

David Helm is deeply committed to the public exposition of God's word and the training of preachers. Yet in this guide he advocates a deep-rooted culture of one-to-one Bible reading in our churches. Surely the two go hand in hand, but many Christians don't know where to start in this personal Bible reading ministry. This guide provides the inspiration for this desperately needed ministry revolution and the growth of the gospel vine into every corner of our communities.

Colin Marshall
Author of *The Trellis and the Vine* and CEO of Vinegrowers

Contents

Part I
What, why and how

I am deeply grateful to Scott Polender for his contribution to the text of part I, and to Robert Kinney for his editorial work.

1 Some people you know

You probably know someone, perhaps a co-worker, who is not really a church person.

Let's call him Andrew. Perhaps you've discussed religion with him; maybe you haven't. You're reasonably sure he's not a Christian, yet he seems curious about your faith. He also seems to have some misconceptions about what the Bible says. You've never had the time or the right opportunity to address his questions.

You also know a young woman at church. Let's call her Norah. She's in her early twenties and recently began attending your Bible study group. She seems to be a relatively new Christian and knows very little about the Bible, but is eager to learn more.

You probably know some others from church—perhaps a young man who is a likable, totally committed

Christian. Let's call him Julius. He, along with his wife, volunteers to help in the nursery one Sunday per month. People respect him and value his input, but he isn't normally tapped for leadership.

These are three ordinary people very much like the people in your life. They each have a different perspective on Jesus Christ and the Christian faith.

Now, let's imagine that you have been assigned to devise a plan for the spiritual growth and discipleship of all three of these people, or people in similar situations. What a task—and where to begin? Perhaps you could invite Andrew to the next big evangelistic event your church hosts. Check. And isn't there a discipleship program going on that might be good for Norah? Check. That leaves Julius. What are you going to do with him? By all outward appearances he is sailing along quite well. Perhaps a special interest class offered by your church might have some interest for him? Check.

Now, if any of those plans for growth were the kinds of things that came into your mind, I want you to know that you are not alone. After all, for generations we have been conditioned to think of spiritual growth mainly in terms of an *event* to go to, a *program* to register for or a *class* to take. The church often puts its creative energy into initiating events, programs and classes specially designed to win people to Christ and help them grow in the faith.

And yet, as successful as some of these plans have been, we might still be missing out on something more dynamic—something more straightforward and right for this day and age—that returns gospel growth to the everyday fabric of personal relationship, rather than relying on church-run programs.

Imagine that there is some way that Andrew, Norah and Julius could all grow in their knowledge of the Lord Jesus Christ by the same means. They could be guided in a deeper, more meaningful way than through an event, program or class. They could be guided on an individual basis by someone who cares for them.

What is this way? What is this activity that is so simple and so universal that it meets the discipleship needs of these three very different people?

We call it reading the Bible one-to-one.

But what exactly is reading the Bible one-to-one? Why should we do it? Who is it for?

2 Why read one-to-one?

READING ONE-TO-ONE IS A variation on that most central Christian activity—reading the Bible—but done in the context of reading with someone. It is something a Christian does with another person, on a regular basis, for a mutually agreed upon length of time, with the intention of reading through and discussing a book or part of a book of the Bible.[1]

1   The idea behind reading the Bible one-to-one in this way is not unique to us or our church. We first encountered the idea in the mid-1990s as it was being used by Carrie Sandom and the staff at the Round Church at St Andrew the Great in Cambridge, England. We also know that similar versions of this idea are being employed at several other churches in England and Australia with great success. Finally, while this idea is typically employed in one-to-one contexts, there is no reason it cannot be employed in one-to-two or one-to-three contexts as well.

In the book *The Trellis and the Vine*, the authors dream about this idea:

> Imagine if all Christians, as a normal part of their discipleship, were caught up in a web of regular Bible reading—not only digging into the Word privately, but reading it with their children before bed, with their spouse over breakfast, with a non-Christian colleague at work once a week over lunch, with a new Christian for follow-up once a fortnight for mutual encouragement, and with a mature Christian friend once a month for mutual encouragement.
>
> It would be a chaotic web of personal relationships, prayer and Bible reading—more of a movement than a program—but at another level it would be profoundly simple and within reach of all.
>
> It's an exciting thought![2]

This simple idea could profoundly influence the growth of the gospel—not only in your own life but in the lives of your family members and friends as well. More specifically, there are at least four tangible benefits to reading one-to-one.

1. Salvation

Earlier we imagined a co-worker by the name of Andrew. Andrew isn't a Christian but he is curious about your faith and, at times, even the gospel message. In your

---

2   T Payne and C Marshall, *The Trellis and the Vine*, Matthias Media, Sydney, 2009, p. 57.

situation, maybe Andrew is someone at work, or a friend, or a family member. Reading one-to-one is the perfect idea for you and Andrew. The book of James tells us that the word of God "is able to save your souls".[3] In fact, apart from God's word to us about Jesus, it is impossible for a person to know how to be forgiven of sin and accepted by him. The apostle Peter makes the same point in one of his letters: "you have been born again, not of perishable seed but of imperishable, through the living and abiding word of God".[4] From these verses it is clear that reading the Bible is infinitely important, not just for Christians but also for non-Christians.

2. Sanctification

Christians are also called to encourage *one another* and build *one another* up.[5] They are called to instruct one another, to speak the truth to one another, to teach and admonish one another with the wisdom of Christ's word, and to stir up one another to love and good works.[6] In his first letter, Peter says the *Word* that saved us is the same *Word* that strengthens us in our faith. He writes: "long for the pure spiritual milk, that by it you may grow up into salvation".[7] In another place, the apostle Paul describes

---

3   James 1:21
4   1 Peter 1:23; see also Romans 10:10-14
5   1 Thessalonians 5:11, Hebrews 3:13, Ephesians 4:29
6   Romans 15:14, Ephesians 4:15, Colossians 3:16, Hebrews 10:24
7   1 Peter 2:2

the usefulness and versatility of the Bible, declaring it to be "profitable for teaching, for reproof, for correction, and for training in righteousness".[8] Christians are called to live *together* as Christians, loving those around them and spreading God's truth to them. Think of Norah and those like her. What does she really need to grow in her newfound faith? Isn't it exposure to God's word? Doesn't the Bible promise us that God will use his word to teach us how to follow Christ? Reading the Bible one-to-one provides an excellent way for Christians to strengthen one another on the road toward sanctification.

3. Training

Reading one-to-one can be used to identify and train people for greater ministry responsibility. In other words, it is the perfect plan for someone like Julius. Most churches are filled with people who love Jesus and are involved in every way that they feel capable. In reality, they are waiting for someone to invest in them for gospel work. Imagine the things people like Julius could accomplish for Christ if someone invested in them for Word ministry. Don't forget, Jesus focused his ministry on teaching twelve disciples, and of those twelve he focused especially on three: Peter, John and James. The message about Jesus spreads today in the same way it spread back then. This investment in just a few may not

---

8   2 Timothy 3:16

seem the most efficient use of time, but it is through just a few people that Christ's gospel has gone out to the ends of the earth, gathering people from every nation into his kingdom—not to mention transforming cultures, fixing laws, founding universities and hospitals, inspiring musicians and painters, and reaching out to the poor and outcast.

4. Relationship

The *personal* nature of reading the Bible one-to-one is another reason why every Christian should consider taking up this idea. In this day, people are hungry for relationships of substance. The language of friendship has become a verb. We 'friend' mere acquaintances with the click of a button. Reading the Bible one-to-one offers the appeal of developing true friendships, relationships of greater familiarity and substance. And it is this personal aspect that appeals to many people. Consider this evidence from researcher Ed Stetzer:

> We asked a total of 1,000 twenty-something un-churched people (900 American, 100 Canadian), and we compared them to a sample of 500 older unchurched (which would be 30 or above)...
>
> One of the questions that we asked them to agree or disagree with was: "I'd be willing to study the Bible if a friend asked me to". Well, among twenty-somethings, 61 per cent said, "Yes". And among their older counterparts of 30 and above, 42 per cent said, "Yes". And that was a statistically significant

difference, telling us there's something going on, there's an openness that's there. So we're seeing that as an opportunity—that in the midst of maybe some negative views of the church, there is also some openness to the things of God.[9]

So, why read the Bible one-to-one with another person? We do so because of our convictions about the power of God's word. When people are exposed to it, they find salvation in Christ, they are sanctified in faith, they are trained for effective ministry, and they find community in a web of relationships that are unlike any other the world has to offer.

9 Ed Stetzer, *How Unbelievers View the Church*, radio program, The Albert Mohler Program, 30 July 2009. For more on this see Stetzer's book (with Richie Stanley and Jason Hayes): *Lost and Found: The Younger Unchurched and the Churches that Reach Them*, B&H Publishing Group, Nashville, 2009.

3 Who is it for?

Before we get deeper into the idea of reading the Bible one-to-one and how it might be done, it is important to understand who it is for. It is most likely that the initiator of reading one-to-one will be a committed Christian, and the other individual will generally be in one of three life stages. We have already considered Andrew, Norah and Julius. They represent these three stages in the life of a Christian:

  i)   before becoming a Christian
  ii) right after becoming a Christian
  iii) a Christian ready to lead or serve.

So the question becomes: do you know people in these stages? In other words, do you know people like Andrew, Norah and Julius?

Non-Christians

One person who might benefit from reading the Bible one-to-one is someone like Andrew—someone who does not have a relationship with Jesus Christ. In fact, of the three life stages we've considered, this one may be the most strategic. Reading the Bible one-to-one with someone at this point in their life will help them come to a genuine understanding of the gospel message and, perhaps, even to make a personal commitment to Jesus Christ.

New Christians

Reading one-to-one is also a good plan for someone like Norah. Young believers in Christ need personal follow-up if they are going to grow in their newfound faith. This time together can help a young Christian develop a lifelong habit of personal Bible study, provide them with accountability, help them to develop much-needed discipline, and instil in them the skills and the confidence to read and understand the Scriptures on their own.

Established Christians ready to be trained

Reading one-to-one will also be helpful to people like Julius—committed Christians who need to be trained for ministry rather than merely being asked to fill gaps in their church's programs. If every ministry in the church should be Word-based ministry, then training someone who could assume ministry leadership will be not only a great encouragement to them, but also an effective way to multiply leaders who can bear more weight for the gospel.

Category	Need	Example	Some People You Know
Non-Christians	Salvation	Andrew	
New-Christians	Sanctification	Norah	
Established Christians	Training	Julius	

I encourage you to write the names of a few people you know and might consider inviting to start reading one-to-one, and then begin praying for that opportunity.

4 How do I get started?

NOW THAT YOU'VE READ A bit about what reading the Bible one-to-one is, why it might be useful and who it is for, you may be wondering how to get started. The first step, as with any undertaking related to gospel work, is prayer.

1. Pray

When God chooses to reveal himself to people, more often than not it comes on the heels of a season of prayer. Luke makes this especially clear in his Gospel. The curious but not-yet-believing crowds were first told that Jesus was God's "beloved Son" at a time when Jesus "was praying".[1] His new followers were called to him the

---

1   Luke 3:21-22

morning after he "went out to the mountain to pray, and all night he continued in prayer to God".[2] In addition, those whom Jesus was training for expanded roles of gospel service—Peter, James and John—caught a glimpse of his full glory at a time when Jesus had pulled them aside "to pray".[3]

These are truths we should not forget. The gospel-writer Luke doesn't want us to miss the fact that prayer is the instrument God uses to ready us for his revelation. To put the importance of this first step of prayer another way: as a consequence of prayer, people will come to recognize Jesus for who he is, they will learn what it is to be his disciple, and they will be equipped to serve him well.

Do you remember the moment in Luke's Gospel when it began to fully dawn on Peter that Jesus was the Christ? Jesus had asked, "But who do you say that I am?" and Peter had answered, "The Christ of God". But don't forget—that famous encounter began with these often-forgotten words: "Now it happened that as he was praying alone, the disciples were with him. And he asked them..."[4] While God saves people through his word, and while he strengthens his people in faith through that same word—even to the extent that he trains us for fruitful ministry by it—he nevertheless reveals himself as a result of prayer. One could almost argue that in Luke's Gospel,

---

2   Luke 6:12-16
3   Luke 9:28-36
4   Luke 9:18-20

whenever the gospel is seen to be taking root and growing, it does so in the soil of previous prayer.

If you want to see people like Andrew come to faith in Christ, and others like Norah and Julius nurtured and trained for a life of service to Christ, then you should begin with prayer. Start by praying that God will lead you to someone to whom he is already looking to reveal more of himself. You can be sure that those people exist, because Jesus has already told us that the harvest fields are "white for harvest".[5] Certainly, there will be someone in your sphere of relationships who knows that you are a Christian—someone who might be interested in reading the Bible with you. Start asking God to lead you to that person.

2. Invite

The second step to reading the Bible one-to-one is both the simplest and probably the hardest. Once you know who you want to ask, you must then ask them. It requires some boldness.

One gentle way is simply to ask, "Would you have any interest in reading the Bible with me for a few weeks?" Now, keep in mind that while asking this might be a scary thing for you to do, it may not be a scary thing for your friend or family member to consider. After all, most people are more threatened when asked to attend a

---

5   John 4:35

church service or program where lots of people might be present, many of whom they have never met. Reading one-to-one is a more personal way to introduce somebody to the Bible. If the person you are asking is a Christian already, then you may want to add something like, "I thought it would give us a chance to get together and learn from God's word".

In fact, the greatest hindrance to inviting someone to read one-to-one will be an unbiblical view that you are not ready for this. You will tell yourself that you haven't been properly trained, or simply don't know enough about the Bible to help another person along the way. In fact, you may even try to convince yourself that someone should be initiating reading the Bible one-to-one with you, rather than you initiating it with another person. It's a tempting thought.

But it's also just not true.

Any committed Christian is capable of initiating a good conversation on a biblical text. In reality, your fears in this area of personal work betray two Screwtape-like lies that every Christian must resist. First, that gospel growth depends on us and on our abilities. This is simply not the case. Our proficiency in the Bible is not the final arbiter in seeing spiritual growth occur. The Holy Spirit can and does use timid people just like us. The second lie we fight against is disbelief—disbelief in the potency of God's word. We need to be reminded that God does his work in his way, and it is his word that accomplishes whatever he desires in the world.

Be encouraged! Invite someone to read the Bible with

you. Rest on the power of the gospel that is in his word. And know that, in the power of the Spirit and through the instrumentality of his word, God will honour your commitment to be in discussion with someone on the message of the gospel.

3. Plan to meet

Third, after your friend or family member accepts your invitation to read the Bible one-to-one with them, set up a meeting to get started. Don't forget the encouraging statistic that 61 per cent of young unchurched people today would welcome this idea.

5 What will a typical meeting look like?

AT ONE LEVEL, THERE IS NO typical meeting for one-to-one Bible reading. We are all at different stages of growth, and will approach passages of the Bible with our own questions and backgrounds and contexts. However, most one-to-one Bible reading meetings will follow a broad pattern, as follows.

Praying and reading

After asking God to help you understand the text you will be looking at during the meeting, begin by reading the Bible passage out loud together. This will influence the place you choose to meet—at times this is effectively done in a restaurant, but not always. Perhaps an office or a living room might be best.

Reading the text out loud together is best done by alternating between the two of you every few verses. If the text for that week is especially long you may want to read only a portion of it before starting.

Talking together

It is very important to employ the art of conversational dialogue on biblical texts. Nothing will kill reading one-to-one faster than when one of the two partners monopolizes the time by pontificating on the text (or worse, something other than the text). The remedy, of course, is to be as good a listener as you are a speaker. Your reading partner will not be challenged or helped if you talk *at* them rather than *with* them. You cannot coerce your reading partner into saying the right answers, especially if they have doubts. It is normal to doubt. You can be a better guide in the discussion if you listen to and acknowledge the doubts rather than brushing them aside or just jumping in with your own observations.

As an aid, remember that questions and open-ended statements usually offer a good way to sustain discussion. The four most important words in a Bible discussion are often *"What do you think?"* (See part II for some suggestions and simple frameworks for having a discussion together over the text.)

Also, don't be afraid of *not* having all the answers. It is not only possible but very likely that in the course of discussion, a question or two will come up that you don't know how to answer. Don't be ashamed, and don't try to come up with an answer on the spot in order to resolve tension. If the question is truly important to your mutual understanding of the passage, then set it aside to discuss at a future meeting. You can always consult study guides, commentaries and even your pastor in between meetings to get a better handle on the difficult questions. But one of the greatest virtues of reading the Bible one-to-one is that it allows people to discover faith in Jesus Christ for themselves, and giving pat answers to difficult questions does not help them do this.

There is one more piece of advice when planning your meetings. Remember to never be so driven in making a particular point or accomplishing some specific result that you miss out on being enriched by the joy of friendship, support and mutual encouragement. Trust that God is at work. (Of course, the opposite danger should also be mentioned—of spending so much time chatting and sharing about life in general that you leave very little time for actually reading the Bible!)

Applying the passage to everyday life

Application is important. Spend some time discussing how what you have read and discussed in the text might apply to your life. It should come as no shock that God's intention in speaking through his word is to change people's lives for the better. As we meditate on God's word, the Holy Spirit applies the passage to our lives—encouraging us as well as revealing sinful attitudes and actions. As we come to know God, we also come to know ourselves more truly.

One practical thing to remember about application is that good applications should always spring out of the text or the context. We shouldn't be trying to apply the Bible in ways that are inconsistent with the text itself. That is, most passages will actually bring up the applications God intends. For example, consider Hebrews 10:19-25. The author spends the first three verses making statements of fact. But at verse 22, everything changes. The author moves from making statements of fact to giving commands that must be applied in relationship to those facts (in this case, *because* of those facts). This pattern is not unique to Hebrews. It appears throughout the Bible and as such it gives us a great strategy for applying the meaning of the text.

Be on the lookout for these kinds of commands, as well as ways in which the characters in a passage are applying the Word as it is delivered. As is suggested in 2 Timothy 3:16, the application of each passage can be for training or equipping a person in righteousness or to do good, or it can provide correction and rebuke when needed. At the same time, be careful not to just woodenly apply any command given in the Bible. Most commands will require understanding of the context—the statements of fact surrounding the commands.

Praying

Conclude by praying again, based on the passage you've read. Allow your thanksgivings and prayer requests to spring from what you've read and how it applies to your lives.

Confirming calendars for next time

Perhaps it could go without saying, but every reading one-to-one appointment should conclude by confirming the next meeting time together.

HOW THESE VARIOUS ELEMENTS work out will depend on a variety of factors:

- how much time you have to meet together
- whether you already know the person well (you may need to allow more time just for chatting and getting to know each other)
- whether the person is a non-Christian (this may change the way you pray, for example, both before and after; in fact, you might even decide not to pray if you think it will be too off-putting for your friend)
- how mature a Christian your reading partner is (this will influence which parts of the Bible you tackle, and at what depth).

The first meeting

Regardless of the pattern that emerges in your one-to-one Bible partnership, your first meeting will probably look a little different.

- If you don't know each other well, you may need to spend some time just getting to know each other better.

- You may need to decide together which book of the Bible to read.
- It's worth taking a few minutes to get out your diaries or calendars and agree on the first three or four meeting times. Make sure you set a pattern that is regular and realistic.
- If you haven't done so already, you'll need to establish the duration of your one-to-one reading partnership. It's often good to put an initial time limit on your reading partnership—say six weeks, or three months, or six months—so that neither of you feel trapped into an open-ended commitment. You can always choose to extend the time later if you want to.
- It's also worth making sure that your reading partner clearly understands *what* you are doing together so that you have a shared understanding of what to expect and how to prepare (if you are going to prepare—see further below). Even non-Christian friends benefit from knowing *why* we are reading the Bible instead of another book, and are often helped by the knowledge that the world is filled with others (like Andrew) who are also just exploring the significance of the person and work of Jesus.

By the time you have done all these things at your first meeting, there may not be time for much Bible reading!

6 Preparation

SHOULD YOUR ONE-TO-ONE Bible partnership consist of simply turning up each time, reading the Bible and discussing it, or should each of you do some preparation in advance?

There are real advantages in each approach.

When both Bible reading partners read through the passage in advance, it obviously maximizes the effectiveness of your discussion together. There are already insights and questions in your minds, and you aren't familiarizing yourself with the passage from scratch. This can be particularly valuable when one (or both) of you are new to Bible reading and might lack confidence.

Some pre-packaged one-to-one Bible reading guides (like *Just for Starters* from Matthias Media) are specifically designed to be prepared in advance, and work better when used that way.

However, there are also some advantages in *not* preparing the passage in advance. It communicates very clearly what is happening in your partnership—that is, you are simply getting together to read the Bible and encourage each other from it. It is not a teaching session (requiring detailed preparation and study), but an opportunity simply to feed from God's word together. And since we trust that God's word is clear and understandable and relevant to us, it is not as if we *have* to do lots of preparation and study to comprehend it. We can simply read it together and hear God speak.

Furthermore, when you don't prepare, you are both starting from the same point—since it is quite common for one partner to prepare in more detail than the other (or for one partner not to get around to preparing).

In practical terms, the decision about whether or not to prepare will come down to factors such as:

- whether you and/or your partner are the kind of person who prefers to prepare and think about things in advance
- how experienced you and/or your partner are in Bible reading
- whether you are using a reading guide that simply works better with some preparation.

This is something to discuss and set expectations for in your first meeting together.

How to prepare

If you are going to do some preparation, agree together on how much time you will invest in this (30-60 minutes is normally enough). The preparation will depend on what sort of approach or method you are going to use in reading together (e.g. whether you are using published resources or some other reading framework, like the Swedish method or the COMA method—see part II). But in general you might follow this sort of pattern as you prepare:

1. Pray for understanding, and that God will use these meetings to grow your mutual faith in the power of the gospel.
2. Read through the assigned portion of the Bible at least twice.
3. Write down your impressions after reading the text each time—observations, main points, questions you have (depending on what sort of framework you are using).
4. Pray based on what you have read, and pray again for your forthcoming meeting.

7 A personal experience

WHILE LIVING IN CHICAGO, I became acquainted with a man who was hard working and highly educated, but who had never encountered the gospel. As we got to know each other over time, we began to talk of spiritual things. He began attending church on occasion, eventually even volunteering to help me with some logistics for a new ministry our church planned to start. My friend remained faithful in this task for many months. After a year I asked him if he had any interest in reading the Bible one-to-one. While he was hesitant at first, he agreed to meet together to talk about the idea. After reading through what was at the time a draft of this present booklet, he decided to go for it. For the next three months we read the Gospel of Mark together in a corner of a local Barnes and Noble coffee shop near his office. He always carried his Bible in a plain envelope—I assume to avoid the embarrassment of being seen with a Bible.

My friend is a trained scientist at a local university. At first, it was hard to keep the discussion on the text before us. He often wandered into the muddy waters of the relationship between science and faith. But over time the nature of his questions began to change. No longer was he worried about whether or not he could remain a scientist if he were to become a Christian. Instead, he began wondering what to make of the authority of Jesus to forgive sins and make man's relationship right with God. For weeks I thought he was close to becoming a Christian but he still hesitated. And then, one week it all just occurred naturally. He gave his life to Christ and I had the privilege of baptizing him into the Christian faith a few weeks later.

What made the difference in his life?

Was it an event geared toward 'winning' him to Jesus? No, it really wasn't. Neither was it a program or a class. It was something more organic, more relational. It took more than a year, but my friend became a Christian. It was the power of the Holy Spirit uniting this man's heart to the truth of the gospel found in God's word, in the context of a simple relationship in which we gave ourselves to reading one-to-one.

It is my sincere belief that this kind of story will play itself out over and over again for Andrews, Norahs and Juliuses all over the world as Christians give themselves to this personal work of gospel witness.

Part II
Frameworks and ideas

I am grateful for Tony Payne's help in compiling this selection of frameworks and ideas.

At one level, if you know how to read then you know how to read the Bible. The Bible is not a magical book, or a book that uses language in a completely different way from all other books in the world. All the normal 'methods' we use for reading things every day are the same methods we use for reading the Bible—noticing the context of what we're reading, observing the words and sentences and what they're saying, coming to a conclusion about the overall meaning, and then considering what implications it might have for our lives.

We do this naturally and without thinking about it when we read a newspaper article, a blog, a novel or a business report. Sometimes, however, we subconsciously leave these basic reading skills behind when we come to the Bible—perhaps out of reverence, or because we think that the Bible is in a different category of literature and not subject to the normal conventions of reading.

Now, of course, the Bible *is* a very different book. Its author is God himself, and its contents are utterly unique. All the same, God chose to communicate his divine truth to us in human language, and his words are written in a book that uses the same tools and conventions of language as any other book.

This means that there is a very real sense in which the ideas listed on the following pages (and the resources listed in appendix 1) are unnecessary. Our hope and prayer is that they will be useful and helpful to you in making it easier for you to get started with one-to-one Bible reading. However, we don't wish to suggest that any one of them is some sort of magic key for unlocking the message of the Bible. The only necessary key to understanding the Bible is to approach it with a humble and contrite heart softened by the Holy Spirit, ready to listen to what God says, and just as ready to obey him.

The ideas that follow fall under four headings:

1. Two simple frameworks for Bible reading
2. Books of the Bible for different situations
3. Help with reading different biblical genres
4. Eight weeks through Mark's Gospel

8 Two simple frameworks for Bible reading

MANY PEOPLE HAVE FOUND the following two methods or frameworks for reading the Bible very helpful, especially in getting started. When you're new to one-to-one Bible reading, using one of these frameworks often just helps you to get into the text and start mining its riches.

1. The Swedish method

This is a very simple, baby-steps framework for people who feel insecure about their ability to start doing one-to-one Bible reading. You could start out with this approach (perhaps for a while) and then move on to the more substantial COMA method (see below) when you have a bit of confidence going.

This simple way of reading the Bible was apparently popularized by Ada Lum, a staff worker with the International Fellowship of Evangelical Students. She named it after the Swedish student group where she first saw it used. It goes like this:

1. Read the passage aloud.
2. Each person then reads back over the passage on their own, and looks for three things:

A light bulb: anything that shines out in the passage and draws attention; it can be something important, or something that particularly strikes the reader.

A question mark: anything that is hard to understand; something that the reader would like to be able to ask the author about.

An arrow: anything that applies personally to the reader's life.

3. Each person should write down at least one thing and no more than three under each category. If you are preparing for your one-to-one meeting in advance, then this constitutes the preparation. Each person should come to the meeting with at least one light bulb, one question mark, and one arrow from the passage.

If you are not preparing, you will need to allow some time for each of you to read back through the passage and write down your light bulb, question mark and arrow. You will need to allow 5-10 minutes for this, depending on the length of the passage.

4. You each share your light bulb/s, and discuss.
5. You each share your question mark/s, and then do your best to work out answers together from the passage (although it doesn't matter if you can't find an answer).
6. You each share your arrow/s, and discuss.
7. You pray together about what you have learned.

As you gain confidence and grow in your familiarity with the Bible, you could expand the range of things you look for or consider as you read the passage. For example, you could look for the central idea of the passage (using a heart symbol); or you could write down the names of people who might benefit if you shared with them what you've learnt (using a speech bubble symbol), with the aim of talking with those people before your next meeting. It's really up to you as to how much you vary and expand the basic method.

The great strength of the Swedish method is its simplicity. It's a very effective way to get started in reading the Bible together, particularly with people who are new to the Bible or who lack confidence in their ability to read the Bible for themselves.

2. The COMA method

As you get more experienced in Bible reading, or if you are meeting with someone who is already a reasonably solid Christian, you will no doubt find that you want to push a little further in understanding the passage. The COMA method is a superb tool for one-to-one Bible reading, both because of its flexibility and because it helps people to integrate their personal Bible reading with the bigger picture of the Bible—the unfolding story of Jesus Christ's saving rulership. As a result, this method helps people to avoid common pitfalls in understanding the Bible. And while it is much more substantial than the Swedish method, the COMA method can still be used easily by people who are not used to looking at a Bible text in any depth.

COMA stands for:

Context
Observation
Meaning
Application

This is really a summary of how we read anything. Even when we pick up a newspaper article, we notice what sort of thing we are reading and how it fits with other things around it (context); we read the words and sentences and paragraphs, taking note of the main events, people and content (observation); we integrate what we've observed in our heads and form a conclusion about what the author is trying to say (meaning); and we reflect on whether the author's message has any relevance for our lives (application).

It can be very useful to follow the COMA process consciously when we read the Bible, because it encourages us to ask good questions of the text and to understand it clearly and thoroughly. When we're reading one-to-one, it also very helpfully directs the conversation. You can work through the four steps together and come to some conclusions, rather than bouncing around with lots of different random thoughts or observations.

A one-to-one Bible reading meeting using the COMA method would go like this:

1. Read the passage aloud.

2. You ask some **context** questions of the text:
   - What sort of writing is this? (A letter, a narrative, a poem?)
   - Are there any clues about the circumstances under which it was written?
   - What has happened so far?

3. You ask some **observation** questions of the text:
   - Are there any major sub-sections or breaks in the text?
   - What is the main point or points?
   - What surprises are there?
   - What are the key words? What words or ideas are repeated?

4. You ask some **meaning** questions of the text:
   - How does this text relate to other parts of the book?
   - How does the passage relate to Jesus?

- What does this teach us about God?
- How could we sum up the meaning of this passage in our own words?

5. You ask some **application** questions of the text:
   - How does this passage challenge (or confirm) my understanding?
   - Is there some attitude I need to change?
   - How does this passage call on me to change the way I live?

6. You pray together about what you have learned.

If you are preparing for your one-to-one meetings, these four sets of questions establish the framework for your preparation. Each person would aim to come to the meeting with something jotted down under each category: context, observation, meaning and application.

One of the real strengths of the COMA approach to Bible reading is that it is so easily applicable to the many different genres of literature that we find in the Bible— Gospels, letters, narratives, poetry, prophecy, proverbs, and so on. For help with adapting the COMA questions for each of the major literary genres we find in the Bible, see chapter 10: 'Help with reading different Bible genres'.

9 Books of the Bible for different situations

THE ENTIRE BIBLE IS THE word of God, and all of it is useful for "teaching, for reproof, for correction, and for training in righteousness", as Paul says.[1] In one sense, then, you can read any part of the Bible with anyone, and derive great profit from the experience.

However, some parts of Scripture are particularly suitable for one-to-one Bible reading with different sorts of people.

---

1   2 Timothy 3:16

1. Suggestions for reading with non-Christians

a. Any of the Gospels

Mark's Gospel is the shortest and punchiest of the four Gospels, and is a favourite of many people for reading with those who are completely new to Christianity or the Bible. You could read through Mark's Gospel using either the Swedish or COMA methods in around 20 meetings, using the sections listed below. (For a modified set of COMA questions especially for the Gospels, see point 1 in chapter 10: 'Help with reading different biblical genres'.)

1. Mark 1:1-15
2. Mark 1:16-2:12
3. Mark 2:13-3:6
4. Mark 3:7-35
5. Mark 4:1-34
6. Mark 4:35-5:43
7. Mark 6
8. Mark 7
9. Mark 8:1-21
10. Mark 8:22-9:1
11. Mark 9:2-50
12. Mark 10:1-31
13. Mark 10:32-52
14. Mark 11:1-25
15. Mark 11:27-12:44
16. Mark 13
17. Mark 14:1-52
18. Mark 14:53-72

19. Mark 15:1-41
20. Mark 15:42-16:8

For a shorter tour through Mark's Gospel, see chapter 11: 'Eight weeks through Mark's Gospel'. This set of readings looks at the key passages in Mark, and provides some simple questions to guide the discussion.

For some other reading guides that take you through the Gospels, see appendix 1: 'Published resources for one-to-one Bible reading'.

b. Genesis 1-12

The opening chapters of the Bible are foundational for everything that follows, and are excellent for introducing people to the big themes of the Bible.

In Genesis we read of God *speaking* all things into existence. Everything we see exists by his word, for his purpose, and under his rule. The climax—the crowning feature—of his creation is the human being. But Genesis also tells us how these created beings have, from the days of their first parents, rejected the very God who created them. Yet while this rejection brings the judgement of a holy God—the banishment from paradise, the flood on the earth, and the scattering at Babel—Genesis is nevertheless a story of God's resilient and persistent grace and promise to human beings, culminating in God's *unconditional* promise of blessing to the man Abraham and his descendants. God has never broken this promise, which is ultimately kept and now available to all people in the person of Jesus Christ.

Here is a suggested path through Genesis 1-12 in eight meetings.

1. Genesis 1:1-2:3   God creates all things by his word
2. Genesis 2:4-25   The first humans: their Creator's masterpiece
3. Genesis 3   The first humans rebel against their Creator's rule
4. Genesis 4-5   The rebellion spreads
5. Genesis 6-7   God judges sin and preserves a righteous man
6. Genesis 8-9   God saves and makes promises
7. Genesis 11   Rejection and scattering
8. Genesis 12   An unconditional promise of blessing

(For a modified set of COMA questions especially for Old Testament narratives like Genesis, see point 2 in chapter 10: 'Help with reading different biblical genres'.)

2. Suggestions for reading with new Christians

If you are meeting with someone who has just become a Christian or is fairly young in the faith, the letters of the New Testament are an excellent place to start your one-to-one readings—not least because many of them were written to people who hadn't been Christians very long.

Colossians, for example, is a brilliant little book about what it means to become a Christian and to continue to live and grow as a Christian. Try reading Colossians over nine weeks, like this:

1. Colossians 1:1-14
2. Colossians 1:15-23
3. Colossians 1:24-2:5
4. Colossians 2:6-15
5. Colossians 2:16-23
6. Colossians 3:1-4
7. Colossians 3:5-17
8. Colossians 3:18-4:1
9. Colossians 4:2-18

Other excellent New Testament letters to read with young or new Christians include Philippians, Titus and 1 John.

(For a modified set of COMA questions especially for New Testament letters like Colossians, see point 3 in chapter 10: 'Help with reading different biblical genres'.)

3. Suggestions for reading with established Christians

a. Romans

At some point in the Christian life, everyone should drink deeply from the book of Romans. This is an excellent thing to do together one-to-one with a Christian brother or sister.

Here, for example, is a suggested break-up of Romans 5-8 that you could do over eight weeks:

1. Romans 5:1-11	Reconciliation with God
2. Romans 5:12-21	The reign of sin to life in Christ
3. Romans 6:1-14	Set free from sin
4. Romans 6:15-23	Made slaves of God
5. Romans 7:1-6	Dead to the law
6. Romans 7:7-25	The function of the law
7. Romans 8:1-17	Life in the Spirit
8. Romans 8:18-39	Future destiny in Christ

b. Psalms

What we refer to as the 'book' of Psalms is actually made up of five collections or books of psalms. The reading plan below covers selections that come from each distinct collection of psalms, with the intention of giving a comprehensive 'taste' of the whole.

As you read the book of Psalms, you cannot help but be moved into great praise of the glorious God who made every part of creation. At other times, you will be led to struggle along with the psalmist over issues of suffering, death, and the apparent prosperity of wicked people in this present age. In all of it, you will rediscover and grow in your understanding of a book that chronicles the songs of God's people, flowing upward to him in the midst of any and every situation.

Here is a suggested reading schedule for the Psalms:

1. Psalm 1	Trees and chaff
2. Psalm 2	The judgement of the Son
3. Psalm 42	A downcast soul turns God-ward
4. Psalm 46	Of God the fortress

5. Psalm 73   Perspective on the end of the wicked
6. Psalm 74   God, defend your cause
7. Psalm 90   A dwelling place for finite creatures
8. Psalm 91   The protection of God's shelter
9. Psalm 107   A history of steadfast love
10. Psalm 110   The coming King
11. Psalm 121   God, our keeper
12. Psalm 148   A litany of praise

(For a modified set of COMA questions especially for the Psalms, see point 4 in chapter 10: 'Help with reading different biblical genres'.)

c. Micah

Micah is a book of prophecy—words spoken by a man who served as God's mouthpiece to God's people. The basic outline of the book of Micah can be found in six words: *judgement now, salvation then, repent now*. The first three chapters address the theme of judgement. The people and their leaders have failed God miserably in idolatry, greed, oppression, and violence. God's judgement will be swift and sure. But then chapters 4-5 bring that familiar promise: the remnant will be preserved under the rule of God's coming king, who will shepherd the people and make them a light to the nations. And the last two chapters illuminate the only appropriate response. The prophet demands that God's people turn to him—not with sacrifices, but with true and sorrowful repentance. It is God who, in 7:18, delights in "pardoning iniquity and passing over transgression for the remnant of his inheritance".

Here is a suggested reading schedule for Micah:

1. Micah 1-2   Against Judah and Samaria
2. Micah 3   Against Judah's leaders
3. Micah 4   In God's place
4. Micah 5:1-6   Under God's shepherd
5. Micah 5:7-15   With God's people
6. Micah 6:1-5   Pleading with the people
7. Micah 6:9-16   Pictures of judgement
8. Micah 6:6-8, 7:1-20 Pictures of repentance

(For a modified set of COMA questions especially for Old Testament prophetic literature, see point 5 in chapter 10: 'Help with reading different biblical genres'.)

10 Help with reading different biblical genres

THE BIBLE IS ACTUALLY NOT *a* book—it is a library of 66 books. And like most libraries, it contains a variety of different types of literature. If we try to read them all as if they are one type of literature (such as one of the letters of Paul), we'll quickly get off track.

Here is an introduction to the main types or genres of biblical literature, and some tips for applying the COMA method to each one.

1. The Gospels and Acts

The Gospels are the four accounts of Jesus' life, death, and resurrection found in the beginning of the New Testament

(Matthew, Mark, Luke and John). They individually cover some of the same parts of Jesus' life, but from slightly different perspectives, emphasizing different themes in the story of Jesus. In a literary sense, the Gospels are narratives. They tell a story (a true story), and as we read them we need to bear in mind how stories work.

Here are some COMA questions that are especially useful for the Gospels and Acts:

Context questions:
- What has happened so far in the narrative? Have there been any major events, characters or themes?
- What has happened just prior to the section you are reading?

Observation questions:
- What do you learn about the main characters in this section? How does the author describe them? How do they describe themselves?
- Is time or place significant in the events that happen in the passage?
- Is there a conflict or high point in the passage?
- Do you think there is a main point or theme in this section of the story?
- What surprises are there?

Meaning questions:
- Are there any 'editorial' comments from the author about the events in the narrative? How do these comments illuminate what is happening?

- Does someone in the narrative learn something or grow in some way? How? What does this person learn?
- What does the passage reveal about who Jesus is, and what he came into the world to do?
- How could you sum up the meaning of this passage in your own words?

Application questions:
- How does this passage challenge (or confirm) your understanding?
- Is there some attitude you need to change?
- What does this passage teach you about being a disciple of Jesus?

2. Old Testament narrative

Old Testament narrative is the 'story' part of the Old Testament. If you look at the table of contents of an English Bible, Old Testament narrative covers Genesis through Esther. Also called 'history', it recounts the story of God's people from the beginning of creation through their many high and low points to their scattering and exile. The narrative passages read very much like other narratives or stories, and so share many of the same literary features: plot, characterization, setting, and the like.

Many of the Old Testament narratives have a particular function in relation to the whole Bible. They articulate the promise of Jesus Christ, the coming saviour. Often through typology or illustration, Old Testament narrative lays out a specific path toward a king of God's people who will both sacrifice himself for them and rule them in eternal glory.

Here are some COMA questions that are especially suitable for Old Testament narrative:

Context questions:
- What has happened so far in the narrative? Have there been any major events, characters or themes?
- What has happened just prior to the section you are reading?

Observation questions:
- What do you learn about the main characters in this section? How does the author describe them? How do they describe themselves?
- Is time or place significant in the events that happen in the passage?
- Is there a conflict or high point in the passage?
- Do you think there is a main point or theme in this section of the story?
- What surprises are there?

Meaning questions:
- Are there any 'editorial' comments from the author about the events in the narrative? How do these comments illuminate what is happening?
- Does someone in the narrative learn something or grow in some way? How? What does this person learn?
- How does the passage point forward to what God

is going to do in the future? Does it prophesy or anticipate Jesus Christ in some way?

- How could you sum up the meaning of this passage in your own words?

Application questions:
- How does this passage challenge your understanding about who God is and what he is like?
- Is there some attitude or behaviour you need to change?

3. Epistles

The epistles are first-century letters, all written in Greek. They make up the bulk of the New Testament. There are two groups of epistles: the Pauline epistles (Romans through Philemon) and the catholic (or general) epistles (Hebrews through Jude). The epistles often contain close, detailed argument, and sometimes it can take a solid 30-minute session of one-to-one reading just to get through ten verses.

The epistles are all written to specific churches or individuals, and the timeless truths they teach about God and the gospel and the Christian life are worked out in these specific situations.

Here are some COMA questions suitable for the epistles:

Context questions:
- What can you learn about the person or situation to which the letter is written?

- What clues are there about the author and his circumstances?
- What was the main point of the passage immediately before this one? Are there logical or thematic connections to the passage you are reading?

Observation questions:
- Are there any major sub-sections or breaks in the text? Are there key connecting words (for, therefore, but, because) that indicate the logical flow of the passage?
- What is the main point or points? What supporting points does the author make?
- What surprises are there in the flow of the argument?

Meaning questions:
- How does this text relate to other parts of the book?
- How does the passage relate to Jesus?
- What does this teach you about God?
- How could you sum up the meaning of this passage in your own words?

Application questions:
- How does this passage challenge (or confirm) your understanding?
- Is there some attitude you need to change?
- How does this passage call on you to change the way you live?

4. Hebrew wisdom literature and poetry

Hebrew wisdom literature (such as Proverbs, Job and Ecclesiastes) and Hebrew poetry (typically referring to the book of Psalms, Song of Songs, and poetic passages found within other books) are somewhat distinct, but are often taken together as a unit—'wisdom' referring to the content and 'poetry' to the literary form. This type of biblical writing is known for its terse style (often using short phrases) and its rich imagery.

Sometimes wisdom literature, such as Proverbs, is deliberately enigmatic and thought-provoking, requiring the reader to chew over the meaning and think in new ways. Its lessons for us are not always simple commands ('go and do this'); sometimes they are observations on the way life works in the world God has made.

Very often, Hebrew poetry uses strong contrasts and comparisons in a two-line form (where the first part of the verse and the second part of the verse parallel each other).

Here are some COMA questions to use with Hebrew wisdom literature and poetry:

Context questions:
- Are there any clues about the circumstances in which the passage was written?
- What has happened so far?

Observation questions:
- Are there repetitions or multiple instances of similar ideas? Do these repetitions make a particular point, or point to the structure of the passage?

- What images or metaphors does the author use? What do they indicate about God or the other people in the text? What might they indicate about modern readers?
- What is the tone of the passage? What emotions is the author arousing?
- What is the main point or points?
- What surprises are there?

Meaning questions:
- Are there specific instructions/commands given to the reader? Does this passage mention any consequences for not following God's commands?
- How does the author motivate the reader/audience, or make his appeal?
- What does the passage teach us about God, and his people, and life in his world?
- Does the passage point forward to Jesus? Is the gospel anticipated or foreshadowed in some way?

Application questions:
- How does this passage challenge (or confirm) your understanding?
- Is there some attitude you need to change?
- How does this passage call on you to change the way you live?

5. Prophetic literature

Many people, even in churches, think that biblical prophecy is mainly about predicting the future. While there is a predictive element in the prophetic books, this is not their primary function. A prophet is one who *speaks for God*, whether about the present situation or the future. The prophetic books are records of God speaking to his people through the voice of a chosen man. God speaks not only of his historical promises to his people, but also of the judgements and blessings they face as a result of their ethical conduct. In this sense, the prophets are as concerned, if not more so, with the present-day moral character of the people as with the future.

The prophets also anticipate the coming of Jesus Christ in significant ways. They often directly predict what God will do through Jesus, and specific attributes of Jesus' time on earth, but they also point to the general interplay between God's judgement and God's mercy on his people in anticipation of the gospel of Jesus Christ. The major prophets (named for the great length of the books) are Isaiah, Jeremiah, Lamentations, Ezekiel and Daniel.[1] There are 12 minor prophets, from Joel through Malachi.

Here are some modified COMA questions suitable for prophetic literature:

Context questions:
- Are there any clues about the circumstances in which the prophecy was given or written?
- Are any people or places mentioned that you

---

1   Lamentations is considerably shorter than most of the major prophets, but is included in the major prophets because it is also by Jeremiah and belongs with his larger prophetic book.

aren't familiar with? (Chase them up in earlier parts of the book, or refer to a Bible dictionary or commentary.)

- Are other bits of the Old Testament mentioned or alluded to in the passage? What part do these 'memories' play in the text?

Observation questions:

- Are there repetitions or multiple instances of similar ideas? Do these repetitions make a particular point, or point to the structure of the passage?
- Paying attention to when the prophet is speaking and when God is speaking, what does the passage tell us about God's plans? What does it tell us about God's character?
- What kind of human behaviour, if any, is condemned or rewarded? What response is called for (if any)?
- What is the main point or points?

Meaning questions:

- Are there specific instructions/commands given to the reader? Does this passage mention any consequences for not following God's commands?
- Does the text have a sense of expectation about something happening in the future? What is to be expected and when? How should this motivate action in the present?
- Does the passage point forward to Jesus? Is the gospel anticipated or foreshadowed in some way?

Application questions:

- How is your own situation similar to or different from those being addressed?
- How does this passage challenge (or confirm) your understanding?
- How does this passage lead you to trust God and his promises in Jesus?
- How does this passage call on you to change the way you live?

6. Apocalyptic literature

Apocalyptic literature takes its name from the Greek word *apokalypsis*—literally, 'revelation'. As such, this genre is an 'unveiling' or 'pulling back of the curtain' on the unseen transcendent world and its role in bringing this present world to an end. This definition is a good beginning, but apocalyptic literature is also known for other literary characteristics, including:

- bold pronouncements that come in picture form
- the presence of vivid visions
- strange and disturbing creatures
- dramatized symbolic imagery
- heavy use of metaphor
- an abundance of cataclysmic events that signal the end of the world
- action that leads to a final judgement and the ushering in of a new world.

While it is very appropriate to focus on future action as we study apocalyptic literature, we should not forget that the death and resurrection of Jesus Christ figure heavily in the events described in such literature. Several books in the Bible include some amount of apocalyptic literature, including all of Revelation, Daniel 7-12, portions of Zechariah and other prophetic books, and even parts of the Gospels and epistles (like Mark 13 and 2 Thessalonians 2).

Here are some suggested COMA questions for apocalyptic literature:

Context questions:
- Are there any clues about the historical circumstances the literature is addressing?
- Are other bits of the Bible mentioned or hinted at in the passage? What part do these 'memories' play in the text?

Observation questions:
- What images are used in the passage? What effect do they have?
- What emotions does the passage arouse (e.g. fear, expectation, awe)?
- How does the passage seek to reveal what God is like? Where in this passage might we find hope for men and women?
- Is there a crisis in the passage? What is the tension/conflict about, and how does it relate to readers?

Meaning questions:
- Are there specific instructions/commands given to the reader? Does this passage mention any

consequences for not following God's commands?

- Does the text have a sense of expectation about something happening in the future? What is to be expected and when? How should this motivate action in the present?
- Does the passage point to Jesus? Is the gospel foreshadowed or looked back upon in some way?

Application questions:

- How is your situation similar to or different from those being addressed?
- How does this passage challenge (or confirm) your understanding?
- How does this passage lead you to trust God and his promises in Jesus?
- How does this passage call on you to change the way you live?

11 Eight weeks through Mark's Gospel

THE FOLLOWING SELECTIONS from Mark's Gospel, and the discussion questions for each passage, would serve as an excellent basis for eight weeks of one-to-one readings with a non-Christian friend or family member.

Week 1 (Mark 1:1-15)

- How does Mark show us that Jesus is worthy of attention?
- What 'witnesses' does Mark call upon to introduce Jesus, and why?
- What is the message of Jesus, and how does it draw your attention to him?
- According to the passage, what has Jesus come to do?

- What is your own reaction to Jesus after reading this passage?

Week 2 (Mark 2:1-12)

- What do you think is the most surprising thing Jesus does in this encounter?
- If someone in a crowd of people said to you, "Your sins are forgiven", what would you and everyone else think of that person?
- How does Jesus demonstrate his claim to be able to forgive sins?
- What difference do you think his authority should have in your own life?

Week 3 (Mark 3:7-35)

- How do people react to Jesus today?
- What responses to Jesus do you see in this passage?
- Why was Jesus' authoritative teaching a threat to the teachers of the law?
- Jesus says, "He first binds the strong man. Then indeed he may plunder his house" (v. 27). What is the point of this statement?
- What house is Jesus claiming to be overthrowing, and what could this mean for you?
- According to this passage, how do you become a part of Jesus' family?

Week 4 (Mark 8:22-38)

- What event takes place just before Peter's confession? Why do you think these two stories are placed next to each other?
- How would you describe the healing of the blind man?
- How good is a partial understanding of Jesus?
- According to Jesus, why does a follower of Christ have to "deny himself" and "lose his life"?

Week 5 (Mark 10:17-45)

- Looking at verses 17-22, what would Jesus say is the basic character of people in the world?
- Based upon this passage, do you think you can earn your salvation by being a good person?
- In verses 32-34, Jesus says that he is going to die. According to verse 45, what is the purpose of his death?
- Read Isaiah 53:5, 10-12. How do these verses help us understand what a ransom is?
- What would Jesus tell you to do if you desired to enter into a relationship with God?

Week 6 (Mark 14:53-15:15)

- When we read of great tragedies in history, we tend to think that we would have acted differently if we had been there. Can you see yourself in this passage? What would you be doing?

- How are some of the characters in this passage similar to each other? How are they different?
- What evidence is Mark presenting in his attempt to prove that Jesus is the Christ, the Son of God?
- How does Jesus' silence actually communicate his identity? (See Isaiah 53:7-9.)
- How has this passage affected your view of Jesus?

Week 7 (Mark 15:16-39)

- How many times does the phrase "King of the Jews" appear in chapter 15 (including verses 1-15)? What is ironic about this? What is Mark trying to say about the events at the cross?
- Read Psalm 22. How does this help you understand the words of Jesus from the cross in verse 34?
- How does Psalm 22 end? What is Jesus ultimately claiming for himself?
- Why do you think the events at the cross were necessary?
- What final description of Jesus' identity does Mark provide? Where have you seen this title before?
- What do the events at the cross teach us about what it means to follow Jesus?

Week 8 (Mark 15:42-16:8)

- Of what fact does Mark want his readers to be sure in verses 42-47?

- What does Mark say happened to Jesus' body?
- What is surprising about these accounts of Jesus' resurrection?
- Why is it significant that Jesus rose from the dead?
- What questions do you still have? Are you ready to follow Jesus?

Feedback on this resource

We really appreciate getting feedback about our resources—not just suggestions for how to improve them, but also positive feedback and ways they can be used. We especially love to hear that the resources may have helped someone in their Christian growth.

You can send feedback to us via the 'Feedback' menu in our online store, or write to us at info@matthiasmedia.com.au.

Appendix 1
Published resources for one-to-one Bible reading

Everything we have said in this book emphasizes that the Bible really is a book you can read and understand—including in a one-to-one context. You don't need someone else to tell you what the Bible is saying. You can simply sit down with a friend and read it together, and hear God speak.

Having said that, sometimes published Bible reading resources can be very useful, especially in giving shape and direction to your conversation over the text, and in helping you to notice things you otherwise may have missed.

Below we have listed just a few such resources from Matthias Media (the publishers of this book). Of course these are not the only good resources available for one-to-one reading, but they are an excellent place to start.

1. For non-Christians

Tough Questions

These simple one-to-one Bible readings work through five episodes in the life of Jesus (in Mark's Gospel). They bring people face to face with the tough questions that Jesus asks of all of us.

The God who Saves

In these five studies, we read a range of passages in the Bible about how God saves us, why God saves us and what we are saved from. The studies avoid the religious jargon that often causes confusion for those from other church or religious backgrounds.

2. For new Christians

Just for Starters

Used by thousands of churches world-wide, *Just for Starters* is regarded by many as *the* Bible study for following up new Christians. It's designed to be used in a one-to-one personal follow-up relationship, in which a mature Christian disciples a new Christian, using the *Just for Starters* Bible studies as a framework. The seven studies are:

1. Saved by God (salvation)
2. Trusting in God (faith)
3. Living God's way (repentance)
4. Listening to God (the Bible)
5. Talking to God (prayer)
6. Meeting with God's family (church)
7. Meeting the world (evangelism)

Matthias Media also produces a self-guided training course that helps people learn how to prepare and use *Just for Starters* effectively to follow-up a new Christian. The course is called *Preparing Just for Starters* and consists of a workbook and accompanying talks online.

Christian Living for Starters

Christian Living for Starters continues where *Just for Starters* leaves off, providing clarity and direction from the Scriptures on what it means to live the Christian life. Topics include: Jesus' return, living by faith, loving like Christ, suffering, generosity, holiness, and living by the Spirit.

3. For established Christians

Short Steps for Long Gains

This is an ingenious and helpful little booklet of 26 short Bible studies (starting with A for Assurance and finishing with Z for Zeal). Each one is based on a Bible verse, with half a dozen questions to stimulate encouraging one-to-one conversation and prayer. It will by no means cover everything on each topic, but sometimes short steps are the best way to make long gains.

The Daily Reading Bible (volumes 1-20)

The Daily Reading Bible series was originally designed as a simple, convenient way for Christians to read the Bible personally day by day. Each volume consists of around 60 Bible readings, with each reading containing:

- the complete text of the passage to be read
- three or four questions to get you thinking
- a concluding point to ponder
- some ideas for prayer.

However, quite a number of people have also found this series very useful for one-to-one Bible reading. It provides a simple and very portable way to read a Bible passage with someone, and talk about its meaning and application.

For more detail on all these resources, including free downloadable samples, go to www.matthiasmedia.com.

Appendix 2
Sheets for copying

To make it a little easier for you to use some of the ideas and suggestions in this book, here are some easy-to-photocopy sheets that you can use either in preparation or in your one-to-one meetings. You can also download these sheets from our website: www.matthiasmedia.com.au/Samples/otobr/ OTOBR-Sheets-for-copying-A4.pdf

COMA questions for the Gospels and Acts

Context

- What has happened so far in the narrative? Have there been any major events, characters or themes?

- What has happened just prior to the section you are reading?

Observation

- What do you learn about the main characters in this section? How does the author describe them? How do they describe themselves?

- Is time or place significant in the events that happen in the passage?

- Is there a conflict or high point in the passage?

- Do you think there is a main point or theme in this section of the story?

- What surprises are there?

Meaning

- Are there any 'editorial' comments from the author about the events in the narrative? How do these comments illuminate what is happening?

- Does someone in the narrative learn something or grow in some way? How? What does this person learn?

- What does the passage reveal about who Jesus is, and what he came into the world to do?

- How could you sum up the meaning of this passage in your own words?

Application

- How does this passage challenge (or confirm) your understanding?

- Is there some attitude you need to change?

- What does this passage teach you about being a disciple of Jesus?

COMA questions for Old Testament narrative

Context

- What has happened so far in the narrative? Have there been any major events, characters or themes?

- What has happened just prior to the section you are reading?

Observation

- What do you learn about the main characters in this section? How does the author describe them? How do they describe themselves?

- Is time or place significant in the events that happen in the passage?

- Is there a conflict or high point in the passage?

- Do you think there is a main point or theme in this section of the story?

- What surprises are there?

Meaning

- Are there any 'editorial' comments from the author about the events in the narrative? How do these comments illuminate what is happening?

- Does someone in the narrative learn something or grow in some way? How? What does this person learn?

- How does the passage point forward to what God is going to do in the future? Does it prophesy or anticipate Jesus Christ in some way?

- How could you sum up the meaning of this passage in your own words?

Application

- How does this passage challenge your understanding about who God is and what he is like?

- Is there some attitude or behaviour you need to change?

COMA questions for the epistles

Context

- What can you learn about the person or situation to which the letter is written?

- What clues are there about the author and his circumstances?

- What was the main point of the passage immediately before this one? Are there logical or thematic connections to the passage you are reading?

Observation

- Are there any major sub-sections or breaks in the text? Are there key connecting words (for, therefore, but, because) that indicate the logical flow of the passage?

- What is the main point or points? What supporting points does the author make?

- What surprises are there in the flow of the argument?

Meaning

- How does this text relate to other parts of the book?

- How does the passage relate to Jesus?

- What does this teach you about God?

- How could you sum up the meaning of this passage in your own words?

Application

- How does this passage challenge (or confirm) your understanding?

- Is there some attitude you need to change?

- How does this passage call on you to change the way you live?

COMA questions for Hebrew wisdom literature and poetry

Context

• Are there any clues about the circumstances in which the passage was written?

• What has happened so far?

Observation

• Are there repetitions or multiple instances of similar ideas? Do these repetitions make a particular point, or point to the structure of the passage?

• What images or metaphors does the author use? What do they indicate about God or the other people in the text? What might they indicate about modern readers?

• What is the tone of the passage? What emotions is the author arousing?

• What is the main point or points?

• What surprises are there?

Meaning

- Are there specific instructions/commands given to the reader? Does this passage mention any consequences for not following God's commands?

- How does the author motivate the reader/audience, or make his appeal?

- What does the passage teach us about God, and his people, and life in his world?

- Does the passage point forward to Jesus? Is the gospel anticipated or foreshadowed in some way?

Application

- How does this passage challenge (or confirm) your understanding?

- Is there some attitude you need to change?

- How does this passage call on you to change the way you live?

COMA questions for prophetic literature

Context

- Are there any clues about the circumstances in which the prophecy was given or written?

- Are any people or places mentioned that you aren't familiar with? (Chase them up in earlier parts of the book, or refer to a Bible dictionary or commentary.)

- Are other bits of the Old Testament mentioned or alluded to in the passage? What part do these 'memories' play in the text?

Observation

- Are there repetitions or multiple instances of similar ideas? Do these repetitions make a particular point, or point to the structure of the passage?

- Paying attention to when the prophet is speaking and when God is speaking, what does the passage tell us about God's plans? What does it tell us about God's character?

- What kind of human behaviour, if any, is condemned or rewarded? What response is called for (if any)?

- What is the main point or points?

Meaning

- Are there specific instructions/commands given to the reader? Does this passage mention any consequences for not following God's commands?

- Does the text have a sense of expectation about something happening in the future? What is to be expected and when? How should this motivate action in the present?

- Does the passage point forward to Jesus? Is the gospel anticipated or foreshadowed in some way?

Application

- How is your own situation similar to or different from those being addressed?

- How does this passage challenge (or confirm) your understanding?

- How does this passage lead you to trust God and his promises in Jesus?

- How does this passage call on you to change the way you live?

COMA questions for apocalyptic literature

Context

- Are there any clues about the historical circumstances the literature is addressing?

- Are other bits of the Bible mentioned or hinted at in the passage? What part do these 'memories' play in the text?

Observation

- What images are used in the passage? What effect do they have?

- What emotions does the passage arouse (e.g. fear, expectation, awe)?

- How does the passage seek to reveal what God is like? Where in this passage might we find hope for men and women?

- Is there a crisis in the passage? What is the tension/conflict about, and how does it relate to readers?

Meaning

- Are there specific instructions/commands given to the reader? Does this passage mention any consequences for not following God's commands?

- Does the text have a sense of expectation about something happening in the future? What is to be expected and when? How should this motivate action in the present?

- Does the passage point to Jesus? Is the gospel foreshadowed or looked back upon in some way?

Application

- How is your situation similar to or different from those being addressed?

- How does this passage challenge (or confirm) your understanding?

- How does this passage lead you to trust God and his promises in Jesus?

- How does this passage call on you to change the way you live?

Eight weeks through Mark's Gospel

Week 1 (Mark 1:1-15)

- How does Mark show us that Jesus is worthy of attention?

- What 'witnesses' does Mark call upon to introduce Jesus, and why?

- What is the message of Jesus, and how does it draw your attention to him?

- According to the passage, what has Jesus come to do?

- What is your own reaction to Jesus after reading this passage?

Week 2 (Mark 2:1-12)

- What do you think is the most surprising thing Jesus does in this encounter?

- If someone in a crowd of people said to you, "Your sins are forgiven", what would you and everyone else think of that person?

- How does Jesus demonstrate his claim to be able to forgive sins?

- What difference do you think his authority should have in your own life?

Week 3 (Mark 3:7-35)

- How do people react to Jesus today?

- What responses to Jesus do you see in this passage?

- Why was Jesus' authoritative teaching a threat to the teachers of the law?

- Jesus says, "He first binds the strong man. Then indeed he may plunder his house" (v. 27). What is the point of this statement?

- What house is Jesus claiming to be overthrowing, and what could this mean for you?

- According to this passage, how do you become a part of Jesus' family?

Week 4 (Mark 8:22-38)

- What event takes place just before Peter's confession? Why do you think these two stories are placed next to each other?

- How would you describe the healing of the blind man?

- How good is a partial understanding of Jesus?

- According to Jesus, why does a follower of Christ have to "deny himself" and "lose his life"?

Week 5 (Mark 10:17-45)

- Looking at verses 17-22, what would Jesus say is the basic character of people in the world?

- Based upon this passage, do you think you can earn your salvation by being a good person?

- In verses 32-34, Jesus says that he is going to die. According to verse 45, what is the purpose of his death?

- Read Isaiah 53:5, 10-12. How do these verses help us understand what a ransom is?

- What would Jesus tell you to do if you desired to enter into a relationship with God?

Week 6 (Mark 14:53-15:15)

- When we read of great tragedies in history, we tend to think that we would have acted differently if we had been there. Can you see yourself in this passage? What would you be doing?

- How are some of the characters in this passage similar to each other? How are they different?

- What evidence is Mark presenting in his attempt to prove that Jesus is the Christ, the Son of God?

- How does Jesus' silence actually communicate his identity? (See Isaiah 53:7-9.)

- How has this passage affected your view of Jesus?

Week 7 (Mark 15:16-39)

- How many times does the phrase "King of the Jews" appear in chapter 15 (including verses 1-15)? What is ironic about this? What is Mark trying to say about the events at the cross?

- Read Psalm 22. How does this help you understand the words of Jesus from the cross in verse 34?

- How does Psalm 22 end? What is Jesus ultimately claiming for himself?

- Why do you think the events at the cross were necessary?

- What final description of Jesus' identity does Mark provide? Where have you seen this title before?

- What do the events at the cross teach us about what it means to follow Jesus?

Week 8 (Mark 15:42-16:8)

- Of what fact does Mark want his readers to be sure in verses 42-47?

- What does Mark say happened to Jesus' body?

- What is surprising about these accounts of Jesus' resurrection?

- Why is it significant that Jesus rose from the dead?

- What questions do you still have? Are you ready to follow Jesus?

matthiasmedia

Matthias Media is an evangelical publishing ministry that seeks to persuade all Christians of the truth of God's purposes in Jesus Christ as revealed in the Bible, and equip them with high-quality resources, so that by the work of the Holy Spirit they will:

- abandon their lives to the honour and service of Christ in daily holiness and decision-making
- pray constantly in Christ's name for the fruitfulness and growth of his gospel
- speak the Bible's life-changing word whenever and however they can—in the home, in the world and in the fellowship of his people.

Our resources range from Bible studies and books through to training courses, audio sermons and children's Sunday School material. To find out more, and to access samples and free downloads, visit our website:

www.matthiasmedia.com

How to buy our resources

1. Direct from us over the internet:
   – in the US: www.matthiasmedia.com
   – in Australia: www.matthiasmedia.com.au

2. Direct from us by phone: please visit our website for current phone contact information.

> Register at our website for our **free** regular email update to receive information about the latest new resources, **exclusive special offers,** and free articles to help you grow in your Christian life and ministry.

3. Through a range of outlets in various parts of the world. Visit **www.matthiasmedia.com/contact** for details about recommended retailers in your part of the world.

4. Trade enquiries can be addressed to:
   – in the US and Canada: sales@matthiasmedia.com
   – in Australia and the rest of the world: sales@matthiasmedia.com.au

Pathway Bible Guides

Pathway Bible Guides are simple, straightforward, easy-to-read Bible studies, ideal for groups who are new to studying the Bible, or groups with limited time for study. We've designed the studies to be short and easy to use, with an uncomplicated vocabulary. At the same time, we've tried to do justice to the passages being studied, and to model good Bible-reading principles. Pathway Bible Guides are simple without being simplistic; no-nonsense without being no-content. Leader's notes are included.

As of February 2017, the series contains the following titles:

* *Beginning with God* (Genesis 1-2)
* *Getting to Know God* (Exodus 1-20)
* *One Life Under God* (Deuteronomy)
* *The Art of Living* (Proverbs)
* *Seeing Things God's Way* (Daniel)
* *Return to the Lord* (Hosea)
* *Fear and Freedom* (Matthew 8-12)
* *Following Jesus* (Luke 9-12)
* *Peace with God* (Romans)
* *Church Matters* (1 Corinthians 1-7)
* *He is Our Peace* (Ephesians)
* *Standing Firm* (1 Thessalonians)
* *Jesus Through Old Testament Eyes*
* *For Our Sins* (The cross)
* *Alive with Christ* (The resurrection)

FOR MORE INFORMATION OR TO ORDER CONTACT:

Matthias Media
Email: sales@matthiasmedia.com.au
www.matthiasmedia.com.au

Matthias Media (USA)
Email: sales@matthiasmedia.com
www.matthiasmedia.com